Mr. & Mrs. Gifts from the Heart

Dolley Carlson

illustrated by Beverly Lazor-Banr

FAITHFUL
Woman

Little book
be on your way

Bless the reader's
heart I pray

Faithful Woman is an imprint of
Cook Communications ministries, Colorado Springs, CO 80918
Cook Communications, Paris, Ontario
Kingsway Communications, Eastbourne, England

MR. & MRS. GIFTS FROM THE HEART
© 2000 by Dolley Carlson for text.

Designed by Brenda Franklin
Illustrated by Beverly Lazor-Bahr
Edited by Julie Smith

First printing, 2000
Printed in Singapore
1 2 3 4 5 6 7 8 9 10 Printing/Year 04 03 02 01 00

Published in association with Yates & Yates, LLP, Literary Services, Orange, California.

Library of Congress Cataloging-in-Publication Data
Carlson, Dolley.
     Mr. & mrs. gifts from the heart / by Dolley Carlson.
       p. cm.
     ISBN 0-7814-3381-9
     1. marriage. 2. Friendship 3. Cookery for two. I. Title.
     II. Title: mr. and mrs. gifts from the heart.
HQ734.C3145   2000
306.81--dc21   99-39105
                              CIP

To mr. Thomas David Carlson
your wonderful smile and loving way
captured my heart all those years ago
and continues to capture it again and again and again!

I love you,
Dolley
mrs. Thomas David Carlson

I am my beloved's,
and my beloved is mine.

—Song of Songs 6:3 (KGV)

Contents

Introduction

"A marriage made in heaven," one wedding guest whispered to another. On a beautiful fall day in New England, my cousin Jennie was marrying Evan. Their wedding moved couples to renewed devotion and gave hope to aspiring brides and grooms. True love still happens!

Everyone wants a marriage made in heaven, but with the passing of time and addition of children, mortgages, and overtaxed schedules, what began as heavenly and blessed sometimes becomes hectic and stressed. Planning something special with your spouse can be overwhelming. You may even think, "I can't get there from here." You can, I promise. Every journey begins with one step, so come with me and step into Mr. & Mrs. Gifts from the Heart.

The ideas within these pages have been put together with consideration for budgets, time restrictions, and the convenience of simplicity. Page by page, I want to encourage and equip you to bring gifts from the heart to your marriage. Edifying gifts of passion, surprise, romance, communication, and good food. (I've included some favorite recipes.) Gifts wrapped in love and tied with a ribbon of faithfulness and joy!

This book was written as a tribute to the Lord, the giver of perfect gifts! One of the dearest gifts is the miracle of two individuals becoming one . . . one heart, one love, one precious marriage.

Let's travel the road of sweethearts as we honor our spouses and our marriages with gifts from the heart.

Once in an age, God sends to some of us a friend who loves in us . . . not the person that we are, but the angel we may be.—Harriet Beecher Stowe

a marriage made in Heaven

you have stolen my heart . . . . —Song of Songs 4:9

"It is now my great privilege to introduce to you mr. and mrs. Christopher Bramel!" The young mrs. Bramel's hand slipped into the crook of the young mr. Bramel's waiting arm, and they walked together as husband and wife for the very first time. Their radiant smiles reflected prayers answered and dreams come true! Tears of joy and sentiment glistened on the faces of family and friends.

Back in the twelfth row, the hand of the midlife mrs. Carlson slipped into the crook of the arm of the midlife mr. Carlson, and they secretly renewed their marriage vows with glances, hand squeezes, and a quick kiss.

now before you gag, I want to tell you that very often mr. and mrs. Carlson arrive at weddings just in the nick of time, and mr. C isn't thinking very affectionately toward mrs. C after driving like a speed demon to get there. As the "time culprit," I'm grateful for the sentiment that breaks the tension between us. But when all is said and done, we are still very much in love after all these years. Our hearts are grateful to the Lord for His guidance, love, and grace.

A good marriage truly is a gift from the heart of God to our hearts, a wonderful blessing of having found a soulmate, helpmate, friend, and lover, the blessing of having found "the one."

For my Love

In the beginning, I couldn't believe
I'd finally met you—The One

Dreaming of, praying for, and wondering about
The One

And suddenly there you were
Your smile, personality, and heart—So irresistible
You became the focus of my time, my love, our future

Remembering brings such joy
Because I love you
And I love us together

_____

_____
(your names)

I so desire to keep our
Love, friendship, and marriage
Fresh, new, playful, and fulfilling.

This is my commitment and gift from the heart
To you and to us.

Stroll down memory lane and recall your own wedding day . . .

The Honor of Your Presence Is Requested . . .

The wedding day arrives at last. Flowers are in place, music begins, guests arrive. Lovingly, grandparents and parents are escorted down the aisle, the groom and his men line up—eyes fixed on the back of the church, bridesmaids enter, and then, escorted on the arm of her beaming father . . . "Here comes the bride!"

The groom can't believe his eyes. He knew she was the one, that she was beautiful, but today she takes his breath away.

The bride sees his love-filled gaze, her heart skips a beat, and though she thought she couldn't possibly, today she loves him even more!

The blessed two stand side-by-side and with holy vows devoutly promise themselves to each other for a life-time of love. As the ceremony comes to a close, the pastor says, "You may now kiss the bride."

Will the kiss be sweet, passionate, shy, bold, or, as I saw at one wedding, will there be no kiss at all (a bashful groom)?

Marriages are as varied as "the kiss"—each unique, but with one ideal and that is to remain in love and married for a lifetime!

Tom and I see the influence of our parents' marriages in our own and know that how we love each other will model marriage for our children and for future generations. Occasionally Tom or I will say, "Who do we remind you of right now?"

"They were just twenty-one and twenty-three when they were married and they could not have imagined what strains the world would put on their commitment to each other, but they believed their wedding vows were not conditional."
—Tom Brokaw in The Greatest Generation

The Bride's Parents ♥ The Groom's Parents
♥ The Bride and Groom ♥

So they are no longer two, but one.—Mark 10:8

Dear Jesus,
We know to plan for the future and learn from the past.
Still, what did Mom and Dad do to make their marriage last?

Broken hearts and broken dreams are in our family too.
Please guide us precious Jesus in all we say and do.

Mr. & Mrs. _____
(your name)

Heavenly Thoughts for your marriage
Think of 3 things that you love most about your spouse. Speak, write, telephone, or whisper all three to your love!

You may now kiss the bride!

Little Shrimp Kisses

Just as the first kiss is a sweet prelude to a lifetime of love,
appetizers are a tasty prelude to the many meals
you're sure to serve throughout the years.
Appetizers are a challenge for me, and I'm saved by
this one every time. It's dainty, delicious, and easy!

Ingredients

A loaf of good quality white or egg bread.
mayonnaise
Tiny frozen shrimp
Finely grated Parmesan cheese. (Boxed is okay, but fresh
   is better.)
Use your favorite cookie cutter or a small glass

Step 1

Use a glass or a cookie cutter for the bread. Cut as many circles
or shapes as you can from each slice. Place on breadboard or large
plate. (Save leftover crusts for bread pudding or to feed the birds!)

Step 2

Spread mayonnaise on each circle or shape, top with 3-5 shrimp,
sprinkle with cheese, place on cookie sheet. Broil until golden—if
broiler is preheated this only takes about 6 minutes. Be sure to
watch closely! Remove from cookie sheet and arrange on a platter.
   Use parsley, lettuce leaves, or an assortment of spring greens
as a garnish around the edge of the platter or just to one
side. Pop in a daisy or nasturtium here and there for surprise!

You must remember this, a kiss is still a kiss . . .
—"As Time Goes By"

Wedded Bliss

There is no more lovely, friendly, and charming relationship, communion or company than a good marriage.—Martin Luther

It's no wonder people cry at weddings! Two lives coming together and becoming one right before the very eyes of family and friends. Two hearts, two souls, two lives dedicated to a lifetime of wedded bliss!

What a blessed assurance to know we are not alone in our marriage, but have the strength of the Lord with us. His loving presence fills our hearts with love and grace. Because try as we may there will still be times when misunderstandings and "attitude" will make our marriage less than holy.

Marriage Prayer

That I may become more like You, Lord, each day
and bring to the heart of my marriage
what You have brought to my heart—
Your gifts of love, grace, and joy.
Please help me to be a generous and cheerful giver
of these priceless gifts
To my spouse and to our marriage.
Amen

Power Plusses, Hearty Helps, and Jump for Joys!

Power—In the frantic rush to get to get out the door each weekday morning, Tom and I pause for just a moment, put our arms around each other, and say a little prayer. It only takes a moment, but that moment makes all the difference! Why not begin your day with prayer together, thanking God for your love and asking for His continued blessing.

Keep company with God. Get in on the best.—Psalm 37:4, tm

Be a devoted student of God's Word and you will be a more devoted spouse.

Once in a while, try to see your spouse more objectively, and you can be more objective about what he needs as opposed to what he can give. Pray for tenderness and insight.

Make me a blessing, make me a blessing.

Dear, Please join me!

Embrace opportunities for attending marriage retreats and seminars.

Always be a student of your spouse.
—Jackie Johnson

Hold your spouse up in prayer. Every time your eyes fall on your wedding ring use it as a reminder to pray for your beloved.

Enter into marriage with a "we're a team" perspective. (If you didn't begin this way it's okay. You can do it now.) God is with us!

A cord of three strands is not quickly broken.—Ecclesiastes 4:12

Leave and cleave . . . You are a spouse first and son or daughter second, not to the exclusion of family, just mr. and mrs. first!

Provide a safe place in your heart and arms for your dear one.

Spend some time reading the Bible; it will be your best resource for life decisions and direction.

Join in friendship with other couples who are "Holy" committed to their marriage vows. You'll be each others' delight!

One boy, 1 girl, 1 heart, 1 love . . . 4 ever!

You can never speak too much of your love and affection . . . joy!

How beautiful you are, my darling! . . . How handsome you are, my lover!
—Song of Songs 1:15-16

Sweeten your relationship with pet names, phrases, and gestures . . . understood by you two only!

marriage, marriage is what
Brings us here today
marriage, that blessed arrangement
That dream within a dream—
may love, true love, follow you forever
So treasure your wife (husband too).
—from the movie *Princess Bride*

Rise and shine and give God the glory, glory . . . Children of the Lord!

The early morning is fresh and quiet and peaceful and . . . it's a hidden pocket of time for a special once-a-month breakfast date and quiet time with your love! An enticement for meeting the dawn could be a really delicious breakfast. This is my sister-in-law Connie's recipe for Rise 'n' Shine! . . . Oven Pancake. We love it, and I think you will too!

Set the table the night before, get out all the non-perishables, and measure the dry ingredients for the pancake into a bowl. This is helpful for those of us who are fairly dazed at dawn. Oh, and the rest of your breakfast menu could include bacon or sausage and fresh fruit. Don't forget the maple syrup!

LINENS

BEDROOM

Rise 'n' Shine! Oven Pancake

Ingredients

3 eggs
1/2 cup flour
1/2 tsp salt

1/2 cup milk
3 tbs. melted butter

Powdered Sugar Topping

3 tbs. melted butter   1/4 cup powdered sugar

Sift flour and salt together. In a separate bowl, beat eggs with electric beater on low. Add flour and salt mixture to eggs in 2 additions (sprinkle over entire mixture) and mix gently. Add milk slowly and beat gently. Lightly mix in melted butter by hand.

Spray the bottom and sides of a 9-10-inch iron or heavy, oven-proof frying pan with non-stick spray.

Pour batter into frying pan and bake in preheated 450° oven for 20 minutes. Then drizzle the center with melted butter, and sprinkle with the powdered sugar. Reduce heat to 350°, and bake for 10 minutes more.

You can slice the pancake in the pan and place pieces on preheated plates for best result. You need to serve this pancake as soon as it is cooked! (PS Connie says this also makes a good last minute supper!)

*Just direct your feet
to the sunny side of the street.*

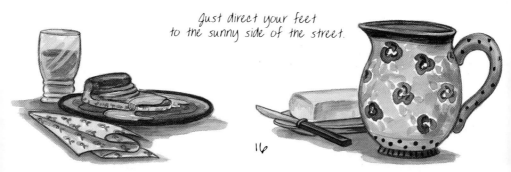

*We'll build a cozy nest, where lovers rest and roses bloom . . .
just molly and me and baby makes three, we're happy in my blue heaven.*
—"My Blue Heaven"

"Home is where the heart is." No matter where you live—
in student housing, an apartment, condo, or house—
home needs to be a place you and your spouse look
forward to "going home" to. The need for a welcoming
home is the same no matter the time or place
or resources: love, a cozy bed, good food, order, grace,
laughter, and joy!

All this and heaven too.—Matthew Henry

Often when there's just no time to cook (or this
cook is really tired) I'll bring home take-out
food rather than eat in a restaurant. Personally,
I love eating out, but I also love the privacy
and comfort of home. We offer hospitality
to each other as husband and wife by serving
each other.

One woman told me, "My heart just melts when my
husband prepares me a meal. It's so romantic and
sets the mood if you know what I mean?" I knew
and know!

Through the years my husband and I have loved our at-home dates. What began as a desire to have time alone as a couple when the budget was really tight and the children were really young (we would trade baby-sitting with another couple, so we could truly relax) has now become a romantic tradition.

Our present desire in midlife is the need to slow down, enjoy each other without distraction (yes, there is romance after children!), and enjoy our home as well. I hope you will be as blessed and refreshed by an at-home date as Tom and I have been. Have a nice evening!

Recipe for an At-Home Date

Offer hospitality to one another . . . —1 Peter 4:9

Extend an invitation to your spouse for an at-home date with the following poem. Send your invitation through the mail, and it will be that much more special!

Carpe diem! Seize the moment!

Just do it!

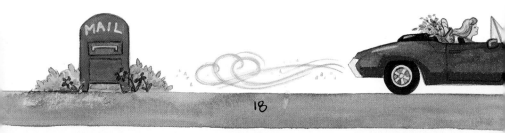

Invitation for an At-Home Date

❤ • ❤ • ❤

I've planned a quiet evening
Just for you and me.

_____
(Insert date here)
I'll make some yummy food and
Rent a good movie!

The house is ours alone
It really truly is
Our kids are cared for too*
I've taken care of biz.

I love you
my dear spouse
And want our love to be
As loving, fun, and spunky
as any love can be.
xxoox

*For other ages and stages, omit this line and use:
There's nothing for you to do

Please, dear reader, if you're short on time and your budget allows, feel free to make creative purchases for your at-home date menu.

A crust eaten in peace
is better than a banquet eaten in anxiety.
—"The Town Mouse and the Country Mouse"

Romantic Movie Selections for Video Rental
According to Tom Carlson, "It's always much more fun to watch a romantic movie at home."

While You Were Sleeping—A young man has an accident that leaves him unconscious, and a lonely young woman tells his family they are engaged. Her tense relationship with his suspicious brother provides classic, romantic entertainment and surprise!

Princess Bride—The story is silly and sweet. Action, romance, intrigue, and quotable lines make this film beloved by all. If you want to laugh a lot rent this video! . . . Two thumbs up—Tom Carlson.

Wuthering Heights—Cathy and Heathcliffe capture your heart with their love found, love lost in this nineteenth-century English drama. Heathcliffe escapes to America, makes his fortune, and returns to claim his love, however . . .

You've Got Mail—Boy meets girl over the Internet. The road to this love isn't direct, but it sure is fun!

Charade—A classic spy thriller/romance from the '60s. Filmed in Paris and starring two of my favorite actors, Audrey Hepburn and Cary Grant.

menu

Assorted Cold Drinks ♥ Beverages of Choice
Hot Tea or Coffee too!

Lucious Snacks
Apple Slices, Cheddar Cheese, and Crackers or
"Just You and Me" Brie Cheese with
Sweet Apple and Raisin Glaze
or
A Platter of Fresh Cut-up Vegetables and Ranch Dip
or
A Great Big Bowl of Hot Popcorn!
and
A Big Bowl of ICE CREAM!

Strengthen me with raisins, refresh me with apples, for I am faint with love.
—Song of Songs 2:5

Sweet Apple and Raisin Glaze

Melt 1 stick of butter with 1/2 cup of sugar. Add 1 medium, finely chopped, green apple and 1/3 cup chopped raisins. Heat just to boiling, and turn down to simmer for about 5 minutes. Pour over room-temperature Brie cheese. Serve with crisp crackers and/or crusty French bread.

21

Set The Table—Set The mood—Ready, Set, Go!
The table setting can be very simple or elaborate.

A candle is a must
Because
A little glow goes a long way!

A candle on the table for every evening meal . . . brings warmth and a sense of well being!

I like to "set" the coffee table because it's not where we usually eat! Even a small change can be refreshing. How about sitting on the floor, picnic style, with a blanket. COZY! Your at-home date could include dinner (home cooked or take-out), or if it's a little later in the evening, some delicious snacks. Don't forget the kisses, chocolate and yours too!

I've provided a list of some of our favorite foods and videos. You provide the date, time, and candlelight!

A woman happy in love, she burns the souffle.
A woman unhappy in love, she forgets to turn on the oven.
—Baron St. Fontanel, in the movie Sabrina

Preheat your heart with warm and loving thoughts.
Keep cooking for a lifetime.
Serve with gentleness, respect, passion, and joy!

Hearts are the symbol of love, and there are so many creative ways
we can express our love with hearts:

- make a heart with his and her initials in the . . . snow . . . sand
- with fingerprint writing on a steamy mirror or . . .
- with shaving cream or lipstick on a mirror that isn't steamy
- with whipped cream on Jell-O or pudding or . . .
- carve a heart on a tree in your yard or . . .
- on your picnic table as one Texan did for his 25th wedding anniversary!
- mow a heart in the middle of the lawn! A dear lady in Alabama says
  her husband does this every Saturday. What a guy!

Reverend Robert and Arvella Schuller decided they did not want
to become strangers within their marriage . . . "not at 1 year, 10
years, 20 years, or ever!" And so, they kept on dating each
other. One night a week for 42 years adds up to more than 2,200 dates!

This is my lover, this is my friend . . . —Song of Songs 5:16

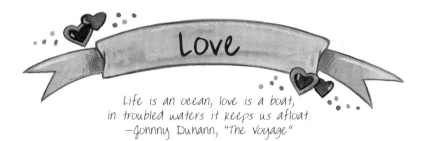

Love

Life is an ocean, love is a boat,
in troubled waters it keeps us afloat.
—Johnny Duhann, "The Voyage"

Every marriage has the potential to be the Love Boat or the Titanic! We need to pack very carefully for this lifelong voyage. Nurturing and caring for our love requires leaving individual comfort and selfishness behind. This makes more room to love, cherish, and serve our spouse.

Whether it's smooth sailing or stormy seas—and you can plan on both—it's our love that keeps us buoyant, but it's the Lord's love that keeps us from sinking. He wants our marriages to be healthy and blessed, not hurt and broken. And He gives us loving direction: "And now I will show you the most excellent way." 1 Corinthians 13:4-8 offers a heavenly list to help you pack or repack for your voyage. . . .

Love is patient, love is kind.
It does not envy, it does not boast,
It is not proud.
It is not rude,
It is not self-seeking,
It is not easily angered,
It keeps no record of wrongs.
Love does not delight in evil but rejoices with the truth.
It always protects, always trusts, always hopes, always perseveres.
Love never fails.

*we cannot cause the wind to blow the way we want it to,
but we can so adjust our sails that they will take us
where we want to go.
—Unknown*

Love Is a Priceless Gift to and from the Heart . . .

Curious, we crowded around an abandoned safe deposit box as
the lid was slowly lifted. . . . Its only content a small piece of
paper. Written in a shaky hand were the words, "I love you."
Words so valued they were put under lock and key! I love you!

*And now these three remain: faith, hope and love.
But the greatest of these is love.
—1 Corinthians 13:13*

How wonderful to know that you are preferred, loved, respected,
and enjoyed, that when you are walking toward your spouse you
are walking toward love.

Blessed, you and me babe, we'll make it through this, "if God is for
us, who can be against us," everything's going to be okay, "come
away with me, the best is yet to be," crazy about you, love!

my heart to you is given:
Oh, do give yours to me:
We'll lock them up together,
And throw away the key.
—Frederick Saunders, 1871

Roses Are the Flowers of Love . . .

Why not plant a rose bush in honor of your love? Water it appropriately, prune when necessary, and enjoy the blossoms and sweet fragrance. Now do the same for your love. . . .

Plant in God's love, refresh each other with serving hearts, cut back when schedules are too hectic, enjoy the look of love in each other's eyes, and "take time to smell the roses!"

You could even select your rosebush by name . . . one that suits you. I bought a moonstone rosebush (creamy white flowers with pale pink-tipped petals) because it's the name of one of our favorite beaches. Have fun!

How do I love thee?
Let me count the ways.
—Elizabeth Barrett Browning

Crazy About You Chocolate Cake!

The time it takes to bake a cake is short and sweet
It's frosting layers, frosting sides, that keeps you on your feet.
So here's a little shortcut to save you lots of time
Just frost the middle, frost the top, and it will look just fine!
Now toss on colored sprinkles and curly ribbon too
And toss on celebration thoughts for your true love and you!

Ingredients

1 box chocolate cake mix
1 8 oz. package cream cheese, softened
1 3/4 cups powdered sugar
1 tbs. real vanilla
1 tbs. of milk
multi-colored sprinkles
3 different colored small spools of curly ribbon

Bake the chocolate cake in two 8-inch layers according to
package directions. Cool completely.

Combine cream cheese, sugar, vanilla, and milk. Blend until smooth (add
a little more milk if too thick). Frost between cake layers and top of
cake, let frosting drip down sides rather than frosting completely.
Scatter multi-colored sprinkles on cake top.

Now cut several lengths of curly ribbon and make curlicues with the
edge of scissors. Alternating colors, surround the cake with "cues" and place
3 more curls in the middle of the cake top just before serving!

"I baked a cake," you'll say to him, "I baked it just for you!"
And your sweet gift will tell his heart your love is ever true.
XXOOXX

He Says, She Says

Oh Lucy, you got some 'splainen to do—Ricky Ricardo

"Honey, honey, did you hear me?"
"Huh?"
"Honey I asked you 3 times . . ."
"Oh, sure, whatever you want to do is fine with me, really!"

This would have been a great opportunity to ask if I could book us for a trip to Hawaii, because I know Tom didn't hear a single word I said. Why? He was watching a ball game, a really good game. If there's one thing I've learned through the years, it's that men are single focused. And when you have their attention, you really do have their attention. My mistake was in the timing . . . . and as you've so often heard, "timing is everything!"

Experience has also taught me that he doesn't need to hear every little detail, he wants the facts. As some have been known to say, "And the point is?"

Jacqueline dear, do not speak unless you can improve the silence.
—From the movie Ever After

Ways to Talk and Be Understood
Ways to Listen and Truly Hear . . . It's All in The Timing!

Bad Timing

When he's hungry
When nature calls
When he just gets home from work (although a
greeting and kiss are essential)
When he's working on the finances
When he's tired
When he's on his way out the door
When he's at work
When he's watching "the game"
When he's reading the paper
When he's puttering
When he has just laid his head on the pillow

Just be considerate, say, "How was your day?"
—Mel Gibson

Good Timing
During a meal
After the children are asleep
In a restaurant
On a long drive
On the beach
On a picnic
Over espresso
In the backyard
In the tub
On a date
On vacation
On a walk

Oh come on walk with me,
talk with me, tell me your stories
I'll do my very best to understand.
—Shane Howard

Ways to Listen and Truly Hear
Have eye contact ❤ Turn off the TV! ❤ Don't
answer the phone . . . let the answering machine do
it for you! ❤ Put down the newspaper ❤ Repeat
in your own words what you think is being said ❤
Communicate as equals

Time must be reserved in marriage for meaningful conversations.
Taking walks and going out to breakfast and riding bicycles on
Saturday morning are conversation inducers.
—Dr. James Dobson in Love for a Lifetime

Fuss & Fume or Forgive & Forget!
Speak feelings, try to avoid anger, sarcasm, old business, and tears.
make I statements not You statements, as in I feel, not You did,
said, or didn't . . .

In their book marriage in the whirlwind, Bill and Pam Farrel give
precious advice to couples: "Life's torrents will come your way. When
the whirlwind hits your home, wrap your arms around each other and
say, 'I will protect you. You will protect me.'"

Love . . . it keeps no record of wrongs.
—1 Corinthians 13:5

Recently at a wedding, my husband Tom spoke about marriage and communication. He came up with a wonderful insight and an easy way to remember its message . . .

Our mates are a gift from God. Every good and perfect gift is from above (James 1:17). We need to be quick to remember this . . . quick!

Communication requires putting the other person first: Everyone should be quick to listen, slow to speak and slow to become angry (James 1:19). So what we have here is quick, quick, slow, slow!

Quick to remember our marriage is a gift from God
Quick to listen . . . Slow to speak and . . . Slow to anger

So when you and your love are doing the country western two-step, remember . . .

QUICK,
QUICK,
S . . . L . . . O . . . W,
S . . . L . . . O . . . W!

A graceful two-step to attentive and loving communication.

From the honeymoon journal of Marie Carlson, my mother-in-law:

April 17, 1938
We had our first dinner — a chicken dinner at a nice restaurant, and enjoyed it very much. We were so happy and thrilled, that any place would have been beautiful and any food delicious.

Communicate Your Love and Admiration

Frame his special certificates, degrees, documents, letters from sports, favorite pictures
Tell your children love stories about their father
Speak again and again of your love for him
Speak again and again of what he does for your family
Speak again and again of what a wonderful person he is, and
Don't ever let anyone speak badly of your spouse, ever!
Kiss hello, good-bye, good morning, good day, and good night!

For out of the overflow of the heart
the mouth speaks.—Matthew 12:34

I've often asked the question, "What is your favorite dessert?" And men always answer, "Cheesecake"!

Lure him for a chat with . . .

"How Was Your Day, Honey?" Cheesecake

Crust

1 6-oz. package nabisco zwieback finely rolled (2 cups crumbs)
2 tbs. sugar
1/2 tsp ground cinnamon
1/3 cup softened butter or margarine

Blend all ingredients together. Press mixture firmly against bottom and sides of a 9-inch springform pan.

Filling

1 cup light cream
1 lb. cream cheese, softened
4 eggs
1 cup granulated sugar

1 tsp. grated lemon rind
4 tbs. all purpose flour
1/4 tsp salt
2 tbs. lemon juice

Add cream gradually to cream cheese, beating until smooth. In a separate bowl, beat eggs, sugar, and lemon rind until thick and light. Add sifted flour and salt; add to cheese mixture, then stir in lemon juice. Pour into crust.

Bake in preheated slow oven (325°) 1 1/4–1 1/2 hours. Cool thoroughly before removing sides of pan.

Serve with fresh sliced strawberries or peaches on the side. (Defrosted sliced strawberries do very nicely too.)

Encouragement

Therefore encourage each other . . .
—1 Thessalonians 4:18

"Hurry, Daddy just pulled up!" When the children were young we had a routine for welcoming Tom home at the end of the day. Candy turned on lights, Katie straightened pillows, and I opened the door, "Hi honey, I'm glad you're home!" Just an ordinary weekday home-coming, but my husband has said many times how encouraged he was by the "welcome home committee!"

no matter what you are doing when your spouse comes home,
drop everything to greet him!—Emily Barnes

One of the most valuable gifts we can bring to our marriage is encouragement. When you fill your spouse's heart with encouraging words and actions there can be no doubt of devotion. It really is the ordinary everyday kindness that makes the mark, the day in and day out considerations. So here are some lists of tried and true "encouragements" just for you!

In our relationships we need to be love finders
not fault finders.—Charles Ara

Encouraging words are gifts from the heart:

- ♥ You're such a good leader ... teacher ... friend ... coach ...
  - ♥ I so appreciate and respect all your hard work.
  - ♥ I love the way you care for your mother since your dad passed away.
    - ♥ How's your heart?
  - ♥ Our children think you're the best!
- ♥ How can I pray for you, honey?
  - ♥ I'm so proud of you!

Encouraging actions are gifts from the heart:

- ♥ Walk side-by-side, not one in front of the other.
  - ♥ Always give the best advantage to your love! As in seat, food, beverage, task, place . . .
- ♥ Turn down the covers early in the evening.
  - ♥ Do a chore your spouse usually does and surprise the sox off him!
  - ♥ Hold hands and each other's cares too!
- ♥ Offer a back scratch or foot massage!
  - ♥ Have a picture of the two of you in your wallet.

Actions speak louder than words

We rejoice and delight in you . . .
—Song of Songs 1:4

At a marriage retreat I heard, "We all have a stake in each other's marriages; your happy marriage strengthens mine." Why not give the gift of encouragement to your friends' marriage: "You two are so much fun!" "You're such a great couple!" "Your love for each other shows and glows!" "We're so glad you're our friends!"

Since you are my rock and my fortress,
for the sake of your name lead and guide me.—Psalm 31:3

"The way to a man's heart is through his stomach," so they say
And my husband's choice would be potatoes every day!
Mashed, scooped, saladed, and souped
Scalloped, fried, baked, and browned
Hashed, right-side-up or upside downed
Boiled, sliced, diced, "They're great!"
And the food of encouragement for my mate!

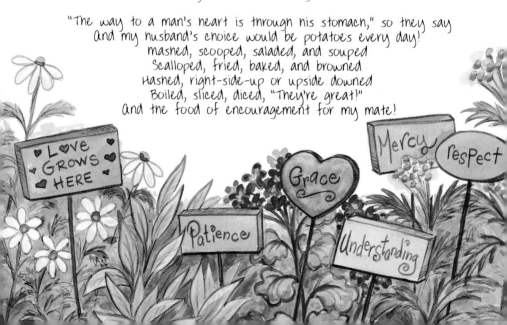

Straight from the Heart Potato Salad

Preparing favorite foods is an act of loving encouragement and reveals heartfelt affection! Not only does this potato salad make my husband's heart happy, it keeps it healthy too! No fat and lots of flavor!

Ingredients

2 lb. small red potatoes
Salt and white pepper
1/4 cup white balsamic vinegar (any vinegar will do)
2 tbs. finely cut spring onions—if unavailable, may substitute finely chopped green onions or finely chopped fresh or frozen chives.

Wash potatoes. Leave the peel on and cut into approximately 1-inch bite-sized pieces. Place potatoes in medium-sized saucepan and cover with water, add a sprinkling of salt and bring to a boil. Turn down to medium-high and cook just until tender. Watch closely.

Gently pour potatoes into a colander or strainer and drain. Place in a large bowl and gently toss with 1/2 tsp of salt, white pepper to taste, vinegar, and spring onions. You may add or subtract salt, vinegar, and onions to personal taste.

I never met a potato I didn't like!
—Tom Carlson

Passion

Place me like a seal over your heart . . .
for love . . . burns like a blazing fire,
like a mighty flame.
—Song of Songs 8:6

The God-created and God-blessed passion of a husband and wife committed to each other for a lifetime is not to be underestimated. Temperatures rise, hearts skip a beat, stomachs carry butterflies, and the pleasure of it all just takes your breath away!

Passion begins not in the bedroom, but in the everyday ways we show consideration and love for each other. When a woman feels loved and a man feels respected and preferred . . . wow!

Just watch the sparks fly!

You're the tops, you're the Eiffel Tower,
you're the tops, you're spring in flower . . .

Acrostic for Passion

Playful—Plan playful and surprising dates for each other. The only expense: thoughtfulness.

Attentive—Remember your dating, falling-in-love days? You listened attentively.

Sensitive—It's tried but true: put yourself in the other's shoes.

Study your spouse—what's important to him and what doesn't matter at all? (Just this morning I learned that Tom really likes for the bed to be made. It isn't always, oops!)

Interested and Interesting—Try to be interested in every aspect of life. Keep the "need to do's" (as in "honey do . . .") to a minimum. Be well informed; peruse the newspaper or watch the news and sports reports on TV each day.

One and only—"We're a team" is what Tom and I have said to each other through the years. This proclamation is especially meaningful during difficult times. Then there's the sweetheart meaning of one and only: *You belong to me, I belong to you.*

Nearer—and dearer—to each other than anyone else, after the Lord. Your relationship with each other comes first, not to the neglect or exclusion of anyone else, but simply first!

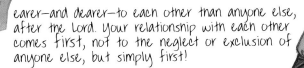

You Take my Breath away!

Love is an irresistible desire to be irresistibly desired.—Robert Frost

mousse
2 cups whipping cream
8 oz. good quality white chocolate cut into tiny pieces
1 tsp. almond or vanilla extract

   This mousse is delicious and friendly too. . . . You make it 24 hours ahead, so that leaves you cool, calm, and collected at serving time!

Pour 2/3 cup whipping cream into a saucepan and bring just to a boil. Remove from heat and add the white chocolate. Gently stir until blended and melted. Empty into a large mixing bowl, stir in almond or vanilla extract, and cool to room temperature. In another bowl whip the rest of the cream until gentle peaks form. Fold whipped cream into the chocolate combo until just mixed—and be sure to do this very gently!

now spoon the mousse into your best dessert bowl, individual serving dishes, or my favorite . . . goblets! Cover and refrigerate for 24 hours.

White Chocolate Mousse

Finish with loving touches!
1 cup whipping cream
2 tbs. powdered sugar or to taste
Toasted slivered almonds
Raspberries or strawberries

Whip cream until softly thickened, add sugar and continue beating until firm but not stiff! Mound and swirl generous dollop of whipped cream on the mousse. Top with several raspberries or strawberries at the last minute. Write I love you on a small card and place it in the whipped cream just before serving.

Optional
Finely crush and lightly sprinkle toasted, slivered almonds on top of whipped cream before topping with berries. Add a little sprig of fresh mint for color.

It had to be you. . . .

41

I am my beloved's and my beloved is mine.
    —Song of Songs 6:3 (KGV)

Where does passion come from, and how does passion grow?
With golden speech, a helping reach, and kind deeds all in a row!

Passion Begins . . .

♥ In the car when you don't complain about each other's driving.

♥ When you make (or creatively purchase) your spouse's favorite meal.

♥ By saying in the most unlikely circumstances and places, I LOVE YOU!

♥ By excusing your spouse from an event he really doesn't want to attend.

♥ By going to an event (when you don't want to) because it's important to your spouse.

♥ By keeping within the budget.

♥ By kissing, kissing, on the hand, shoulder, top of head, lips. Little kisses and big kisses!

♥ By tenderly carrying each other through disappointments and broken dreams to "The Sea of Love," understanding, and hope.

♥ By tending to all the family's needs when the other spouse is exhausted.

♥ By speaking nicely, respectfully, and affectionately (not too mushy in public) to your spouse.

♥ By—and this is so cliché but true—wearing something nice to bed. And if you don't have anything nice to wear, don't wear anything!

Passion, red-hot, sizzling passion
begins with true love!

Playfulness

"all work and no play makes Jack a dull boy"
and Jill isn't too happy either!

Sometimes in our earnestness to do life right, we forget to play!
When was the last time you and your love played?
If you can't remember, well . . . . it's playtime!

a marriage survey asked husbands what they wanted
most from their wives. When I ask women how they think
the men answered, they always exclaim, "Sex!" Good answer,
but not *the* answer. most men answered PLAYFULNESS!
Who would have guessed?

Hello young lovers, whoever you are.—The King and I

Observe young lovers . . . . they're full of playfulness!
Tom and I were on a date, and I noticed a college couple
just ahead of us. Suddenly the girl said to the boy,
"Race you!" He responded with a huge grin and began
running. Recalling that "playfulness" statistic, I said to
Tom Carlson, "Race you!" and began running. He did too!
who won? We both did because we were "in the moment"
and spontaneously played! Spontaneity is the key to
initiating and responding to playfulness.

43

Not long ago, three young wives told me their plans for a Valentine's date. Instead of expecting their husbands to plan a romantic evening, they surprised them with an evening at a park—miniature golf, batting cages, games, and bumper cars! Gifts from the heart of loving consideration and playfulness too!

To a young heart everything is fun.—Charles Dickens

Grounds for Playfulness

Swing in the swings at a park. ❤ Go swimming and have a splash fight! ❤ Buy ice-cream cones, take a walk . . . grab his cone and run! ❤ Pause by a water fountain and when he takes a drink . . . turn the faucet up and get ready for his playful revenge! ❤ If your clothing is washable . . . kick off your shoes and jump fully clothed in the shower with him . . . just for a while, fully clothed that is! ❤ Kiss in the car when you reach your destination or in front of your house, a little or a lot!

His left arm is under my head,
and his right arm embraces me.
—Song of Songs 2:6

Put a squeaky toy between the mattress and box spring
on his side of the bed; pretend to be asleep while he's trying
to figure out where that sound is coming from!
Play an old-fashioned game of jacks, marbles, monopoly,
pick-up sticks, or "go fish."
Sleep under the stars in your backyard. . . .
Set up sleeping bags and air mattresses ahead of time.
When it's time for bed, surprise him.
Don't forget the flashlights!

*Are the stars out tonight? I don't care if it's cloudy or bright—
"cause I only have eyes—for you, dear.*

Put glow-in-the-dark stars on the ceiling over your bed. I did this
as a surprise for Tom, and when the lights were out he couldn't believe
his eyes! Now almost every night he says, "Honey, the stars are out
tonight!" Walk in the rain and splash in the puddles!
Walk in the fall leaves and kick up your heels!
Make angels in the snow.
Go sledding with your playmate.
Throw snowballs!
Build a snowman or lady
or mr. & mrs.!

Roll down all the windows in the car and show him
you don't care about your hair!

❀

Stop the ice-cream man and buy *Bomb Pops, Dreamsicles,*
or *Nutty Drumsticks.* Sit on the curb and enjoy!

❀

Go for a bike ride, but first clip a baseball card to the
wheel so it flips against the spokes and makes the
sound of HAVING FUN!

❀

Better yet borrow or rent a "rag top" (convertible), pop in a "music
when you were falling in love" tape or CD, and commit a morning,
afternoon, or day to a drive with your honey!

❀

Buy two paddleboards, the kind where a small ball is
attached to elastic and you pong, pong, pong!
See who can do the most pongs in a row!

❀

Walk on top of a (not too tall) wall and balance with your arms extended
. . . whoops!

❀

Rollerblade and be sure to wear all the protective gear!

❀

Shoot hoops! . . . Bat balls! . . . Toss a volleyball.

❀

Build a sandcastle or a fort!

❀

Go down a slide
. . . wheeeeeeeeeee!

you & me

Play Hide-and-Seek!

I don't remember how this got started, but we have a small soft lamb, and we hide that little guy in unexpected places. I find it, Tom finds it— in dresser drawers, bathroom cabinets, shoes, under the pillow, in a suitcase (not a briefcase—could be embarrassing in front of the boss), under a cap, in a purse, in a jacket pocket, you just never know where it will show up! The point being . . . playfulness and I'm thinking of you! By the way we never talk about the little lamb . . . just hide him in new places!

I will search for the one my heart loves.
—Song of Songs 3:2

Play . . .
In the moment
For the day
In the evening
Play!

Play . . .
Laugh and giggle
Sing and dance
It can lead to such romance
Play!

Play . . .
Tag and jump rope
Hide-and-seek
For a weekend or a week
Just PLAY!

A happy heart makes the face cheerful.
—Proverbs 15:13

47

"Throw the Rice" . . . Pudding

In honor of playfulness and an old-fashioned wedding tradition I have renamed one of my favorite recipes—"Throw the Rice" . . . Pudding.

This favorite comes from Tom's grandmother Tillie Onlund. It's easy to prepare and so good! Grandma Onlund also had a very good recipe for marriage. She had been married for 49 years when Grandpa went home to heaven! "Honey, men like to be admired, loved, and most of all respected." This recipe is easy. All you need is love.

> 3/4 cup uncooked rice
> 2 cups water
> 2 tbs. butter

Melt butter, add water and rice and bring to a boil. Immediately reduce heat to medium. Cook for 15 or 20 minutes or until water is absorbed, stirring occasionally.

> 1 quart milk
> 4 or 5 large eggs
> 1 tsp. vanilla
> 1/2 cup sugar

Beat eggs. Add sugar, milk, and rice. Pour into casserole and sprinkle with nutmeg. Bake uncovered at 350° for 1 to 1 1/4 hours, or just until knife comes out clean.

Lingonberries make a very tasty and tart accompaniment to this pudding which can be served as dessert (add a bit of sweetened whipped cream for this) or as a side dish with meat.

Romance

I found the one my heart loves. I held him and would not let him go.
—Song of Songs 3:4

"Actions speak louder than words," we're told, and I believe they do! When Tom and I were dating, he invited me to his parents' home for Sunday dinner. It was joyous chaos, adults, children, grandchildren around the table, food being passed back and forth, laughter, stories, and Tom's dear parents at the helm of it all!

In the midst of the pandemonium, I glanced at Mr. and Mrs. Carlson only to see Tom's mother (when she thought no one was looking) quickly kiss her husband's shoulder. That little kiss showed a young lady who was falling in love with their son that love lived in this family. Not too much later I said yes to Tom's "Will you marry me?" You could say my answer had been sealed with that romantic Sunday afternoon kiss!

We don't think of a dining room as the most romantic setting, but it was! Tom's mother learned early in her marriage to "seize the moment" for romance . . . no waiting . . . just quick thinking and quick kisses!

What's the most romantic word in marriage? Commitment! When you enter marriage with a forever mind and heart, it strengthens your bond and creates tremendous confidence and a sense of protection in and for each other. My parents, Rita and Robert, courted and were married in the 1940s. They selected one of the most romantic songs of that time as "our song." They're gone now, but every time I hear their song I picture them as they were—young, glowingly in love, and committed to loving each other always.

I'll be loving you always—
with a love that's true, always—
. . . not for just an hour, not for just a day,
not for just a year, But always—always.
—I'll Be Loving You Always

Linda Smith, a dear friend who has been married for 30 years, says, "Commitment is what gets you through when crazy-in-love is not there due to life's ups and downs and stresses."

Friends were given a gift certificate for a weekend away at a posh hotel by the husband's parents who also offered to baby-sit! But the wife just didn't want "to leave the children for a whole weekend." I said, "Call your mother-in-law right now, thank her, and make arrangements. Your children need a break too, and it's a lot of fun to spend time with Grandma and Grandpa!"

my friend Carol (very happily married for 47 years) said it all when she commented on parents who won't take time for dates: you need to celebrate the love that created those children.

Romance in marriage

Often ladies will say, "my husband just isn't romantic, and I'm tired of being the only one who makes anything romantic happen in our marriage." If this is your experience I want to validate your frustration, but I also want to encourage you.

Some men just aren't comfortable with "hearts and flowers" but show their love in very practical ways such as . . . responding to your concern about a wall that needs painting, a lawn that needs mowing, a squeaky gate that needs oiling . . . get the picture! He loves you and this is his way of romancing!

The Circle of Endearment

If you stop romancing your marriage . . . then what . . . no romance at all? Your loving ways inspire his way of loving and his way of loving inspires your loving him and a circle of endearment has begun. If you stop romancing you'll find your hearts stuck at the intersection of won't, should, comparison, and disappointment! Keep romancing your husband, this is your love, your life companion, the man who loved you so much he asked you to spend the rest of your life with him. And you said to your girlfriends, "Guess what? I'm getting married!"

Wash and perfume yourself, and put on your best clothes.
—Ruth 3:3

How we look, how we smell, and how we're dressed contribute greatly to romance. I'm not talking about the latest style or elaborate grooming, just being fresh and sweet in anticipation of spending time with your love.

Kiss, n. A word invented by the poets
as a rhyme for "bliss."
—Ambrose Bierce

While shopping I ran into my friend Kari buying a robe and slippers because she and her husband were going away for the weekend. "Dolley, my robe had that gross mark right across the middle, the one you get from doing the dishes and a little housework before getting dressed. And my slippers . . . . don't get me started!"

Whether we shop uptown or downtown, just getting new intimate clothing can be very romantic. It shows your love that you care and well, let me put it this way, it's an enticing invitation . . . . to romance!

Clothe yourselves with compassion, kindness, humility, gentleness and patience. . . . And over all these virtues put on love, which binds them all together in perfect unity.—Colossians 3:12, 14

You can have a romantic weekend away even if the budget is tight. When our children were young, Tom's parents would come to our home and look after our girls while we went to their home. Yes, you can be romantic in your parents' home. . . . They just need to be someplace else! If you're the grandparent, maybe this is a gift from the heart you'd like to give to your children and grandchildren. Our girls are young adults now, but they still remember these wonderful times with Grandma and Grandpa.

or have a romantic weekend away . . . at home. Trade baby-sitting with another couple and dedicate your weekend to romance, playfulness, and joy! no work or projects or tele-phone calls allowed. . . . You're being held captive by love for each other and unavailable. Remember, you're away . . . at home!

maybe a whole weekend isn't possible, but you can still have romance . . . plan a date!

a couple we know was about to go on their weekly date when one of their four children began crying, hysterically. They knew this was more than the routine separation cry, and it looked as if the baby-sitter was about to quit, so they told their four-year-old son he could come with them, but he needed to be on his best behavior. . . . The maitre 'd of the sophisticated french restaurant was a bit huffy about seating the little boy in his red flannel pajamas!

I'm not recommending this, but it does show commitment . . . to romance and keeping a date and loving your mate!

Out-of-the-ordinary communications contribute greatly to the "spice" in our marriages! My husband and I had decided to use our cell phone "strictly for business or an emergency." However, one afternoon I phoned him just to whisper something very romantic. He coolly responded, "Can I get back to you on that?" And then it occurred to me . . . "Oh, oh honey, you're not alone!" And he replied, "You're absolutely right!" Unknown to me he always used the speaker-phone when driving, but thank goodness he didn't this time . . . because his boss was in the car! We have more fun remembering that afternoon and how close we came to being soooooooooo embarrassed! "Ummm, sweet nothin's."

Kiss me once, and kiss me twice,
and kiss me once again. . . .

Following my Romance in marriage talk, we often have discussion. One question is, "What gift is on his list that only you could surprise your husband with?" A young wife and mother answered, "Well, he's been wanting the Lego pirate ship for a long time." Her friend said, "No that's not what the question means. I think you can still get the pirate ship, you just need to get in a bubble bath and be holding it for him!"

She got it!

His   Hers

Romantic Ideas

Send a telegram, letter, greeting card, e-mail saying, "I love you." 🐝 Take a bubble bath together. Fill the room with candles. 🐝 Serve dinner in your bedroom and have little hearts or notes leading the way! 🐝 Put love notes in his workshop, office, briefcase, or car for him to find throughout the day. 🐝 When you're sitting in a meeting, lean over and write "I love you" or something endearing or something inviting on his notes! 🐝 Have a "during the week" picnic at sunset. 🐝 Phone your love on Tuesday—ask for a date on Saturday and don't tell where you're going. 🐝 Write a love letter (a long one) send it special delivery. 🐝 A wonderful breakfast in bed! 🐝 Air kiss across a crowded room . . . lips pursed for a millisecond! 🐝 When we have name tags or place cards from an event I put them on display side by side for a few weeks—just love to see mr. & mrs. in writing! 🐝 Tuck a passionate little note in the pocket of his favorite jacket, pants, or shirt. Put one in each of a pair of socks, and he'll walk through the day with a grin! 🐝 Put this down and kiss, hug, and celebrate your love!

We seldom leave town without a basket full of goodies. It just makes everything more enjoyable and relaxing. It's romantic to pack your best . . . napkins, mugs, pretty paper napkins and paper plates (not the 100 for 50 cents variety unless you're going camping). Remember this is the love of your life! If you were dating and looking at your husband as a potential husband only the best would do! Well, he's here now and he is your husband. Cherish him, make him feel like a king, romance him. . . .

> Take me away with you—let us hurry!
> —Song of Songs 1:4

Surprise, surprise, surprise! Do the absolute unexpected. A limo? Theater tickets? Kidnap for a weekend—or evening—adventure. A hot air balloon ride? A day at the beach or amusement park or aquarium or zoo!

> Let me call you sweetheart,
> I'm in love with you.

"Just the Two of Us"
Weekend Getaway Basket

A votive candle (don't forget the matches) ♥ Pretty napkins and paper plates ♥ Two sets of plastic knives, forks, and spoons ♥ Two small goblets—the real thing—no plastic ♥ Two coffee mugs—the real thing—again! (Buy inexpensive ones. If they break, they break. This is your love and he's worth it!) ♥ A small, travel electric tea kettle

Cookies ♥ Chips and salsa
Crackers ♥ Fresh fruit
Candy ♥ Boxed fruit drinks
Sparkling water, plain and flavored too
A package of cheese

We also bring Danish pastries from our local bakery for a leisurely breakfast on the first day of our getaway! ♥ Tea bags or . . . fancy instant coffee drink and a can of whipped cream. The whipped cream, cheese, and salsa can be insulated until you get to your destination, then put them in your hotel room fridge or keep cool with ice.

Be playful . . .
and don't forget the whipped cream!

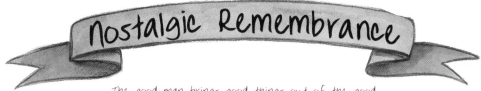

Nostalgic Remembrance

The good man brings good things out of the good stored up in his heart.—Luke 6:45

"So how did you two meet?" My husband always begins his answer with, "For me it was love at first sight." I love to hear him say it! It's so dear to remember the beginning of your love for each other. On and for me, it all began with Tom's smile, his wonderful, wonderful smile! What was it for you?

Some enchanted evening you may meet a stranger.

Remember, remember what first attracted you to each other. . . . now kiss and tell! Remember what you used to do for fun and do it again! Maybe you took long walks on the beach or browsed through bookstores or hiked or biked or maybe you had a favorite picnic spot or restaurant. All those things that lovers do. Even if these things are geographically or financially challenging presently, improvise or just remember together. It's fun!

He simply went to a place in my heart that was waiting for him.
—from 1940s movie, King's Row

Memory Lane

Our friend Peter gave his wife, Gail, a nostalgic remembrance gift for their twenty-fifth wedding anniversary.

"When we were in college I took Gail to a charming country restaurant and it was one of our first really romantic times." As he repeated *really romantic times*, I heard the voice of the smitten young man. . . .

Years later he called that same restaurant to make reservations for a surprise anniversary dinner, and the owner said it was the only night of the week they weren't open! When Peter told him it was their twenty-fifth anniversary and that it all began there, the owner insisted on opening the restaurant for JUST THE TWO OF THEM that evening!

Gail was bubbling as she recalled the details. Not only did I hear the voice of the **smitten** young man, I heard the glee of a young woman falling in love!

> The heart that loves is always young.—Greek Proverb

Why not fall into nostalgic remembrance with your love this weekend. It needn't be elaborate, just thoughtful.

> Two souls with but a single thought,
> Two hearts, that beat as one.—Friedrich Halm

Just Remember . . .

Keep a simple journal of everyday ways you express your love to each other.

Keep a photo album with the same intent—your everyday life as opposed to special occasions. Some friends showed us an album from their first year of marriage. My favorite picture was of them at the kitchen table for a weekday meal.

One lady bought two large gold frames and made collages from all the greeting cards her husband had given her throughout their 30-year marriage. It was beautiful!

Create a collection of all your favorite love songs on one tape and surprise your love by playing it without announcement. Oh, they're playing our song, and our other song, and . . . can you believe this!

He gave you violets . . . oh my,
only a very nice young man would select violets.
They're so old fashioned.
My grandmother said this of my beau who is now my husband.

Save a favorite piece of clothing from your dating days. If it's too late . . . go to a vintage shop and try to duplicate it. If it's really cute, wear it on a date! Although I didn't intend to do this,—I love that it happened—I still have the dress I wore on my first date with Tom. It's a classic little black dress, and now my daughters wear it!

Refresh your marriage with yesterday's memories and today's surprises!
Better yet, why not put together a romantic Italian dinner party and ask
everyone to bring something for the dinner, but more importantly . . .
their love story!

An Evening in Italy
Dinner Party

Menu

Italian Sparkling Water or Beverage of Choice

Antipasto
A Plate of Sliced Salami, Provolone Cheese, Peppers & Olives
Served with Crusty Italian Bread, Olive Oil & Vinegar

Green Salad with Italian Dressing

Ti Amo Fettuccini
&
Freshly Grated Parmesan Cheese

Dessert
Spumoni Ice Cream & Italian Cookies
Cappuccino

Candlelight

Italian Music
(Andrea Bocelli's Romanza CD is so . . . romantic!)

when the moon hits your eye
like a big pizza pie,
that's amore!

Ti Amo Fettuccini

Fettuccini pasta for six

8 boneless, skinless chicken breasts, cut into bite-sized pieces
10 fresh tomatoes
Chopped crushed garlic—to taste (ready made in jar)
1/2 to 1 cup of fresh, chopped basil (more or less according to taste)
Olive oil—add more or less to taste
Salt and pepper to taste

Heat moderate amount of olive oil in a large frying pan. Add chopped chicken, salt, and pepper to taste. When chicken is golden, add tomatoes and garlic, gently stir until cooked through. Stir in basil at last minute and cook for a short time (cook too long and it will be bitter).

Meanwhile cook fettuccini according to package directions (fresh fettuccini is even better if you know a deli close by that makes it). Drain cooked pasta in a colander or strainer. Pour into a large pasta bowl, add chicken and tomato, gently stir. Serve with freshly grated parmesan cheese (fresh makes all the difference!)

Buon Appetito!

At evening's end, say arrivederci to your guests, close the door, turn up the music, kiss your husband, and turn off the porch light!

A
Benediction
of Love and Blessing
for your marriage

May God go before you to guide you
Above you to watch over you
Behind you to encourage you
Within your hearts with His love and peace
And beside you as the third strand in the cord of three
The blessed, strong, and joyous cord of wedded bliss.

Let love and faithfulness never leave you;
bind them around your neck, write them on the tablet
of your heart.—Proverbs 3:3

God send His joy and love and light
To make your wedded pathway bright
And may His goodness ever bless
Your lives and home with happiness.

Dolley